01

Ve rian

ISBN 1 74022 507 4
Published by R&R Publications Marketing Pty Ltd
ABN 78 348 105 138
PO Box 254, Carlton North, Victoria 3054 Australia
Phone: (61 3) 9381 2199, Fax: (61 3) 9381 2689
Australia-wide tollfree 1800 063 296
E-mail: info@randrpublications.com.au
Web: www.randrpublications.com.au
Publisher: Richard Carroll
Production Manager: Anthony Carroll
Cover Designer: Aisling Gallagher
Layout Designer: Elain Wei Voon Loh
Recipes: Concept New Zealand & R&R Kitchens
Photography: Concept New Zealand & R&R Kitchens
Proofreading: Holly Alexander

Printed in Singapore

Contents

Introduction

Eating less meat and fish by substituting more grains, beans and vegetables has become increasingly popular in recent years.

This book presents a selection of imaginative recipes for those who delight in the vegetarian menu. The recipes in this book have been developed using the most imaginative techniques to ensure that the reader will delight in the taste sensations produced by the most simple fare.

Fresh, light, delicious – these are not words that many people associate with vegetarianism. That is, until now. Vegetarianism has, for far too long, been associated in people's minds with 'gluggy' bowls of brown rice, plates of boiled lentils, indigestible slabs of 'good-for-you' pies which, rather than being feather-light and delectable, sit in your stomach for hours. Banish those ideas forever.

The influence of Asian cooking styles, such as stir-frying and steaming, have been eagerly embraced by imaginative vegetarian cooks, with the result that vibrantly coloured vegetables, stir-fried in a trice, sprinkled with fresh coriander leaves and accompanied by a little steamed Basmati rice are winning over traditional meat eaters.

Today, people are increasingly turning to delicious, inexpensive and healthy vegetarian fare as an alternative to the traditional meaty mains. Whether you want occasional meatless meals or a completely vegetarian diet, you will find many imaginative suggestions in this beautifully photographed book.

More than ever before, people want to experience their natural energy, and to simply feel 'good'. Light, meatless eating is one widely acknowledged way to achieve this goal.

Well-balanced vegetarian diets are now known to be nutritionally adequate, especially those that include milk and eggs. Very severe diets can be a problem, although with careful planning these too can be nutritionally sound. Strict macrobiotic or fruitarian (fruit only) diets cannot provide all the nutrients you need for good health.

Garlic and parsley soup

1 head garlic, cloves separated and unpeeled

6 cups vegetable stock

1/4 teaspoon dried sage

1/4 teaspoon dried thyme

1 small bay leaf

3 sprigs fresh parsley

2 large potatoes, diced

pinch saffron powder

1 bunch fresh parsley, finely chopped

freshly ground black pepper

Serves 6

1 Bring a saucepan of water to the boil, add garlic cloves and boil for 30 seconds. Drain, rinse under cold water and peel.

2 Place garlic, stock, sage, thyme, bay leaf and parsley sprigs in a large saucepan and bring to the boil. Reduce heat and simmer for 30 minutes.

3 Add potatoes and saffron to stock mixture and simmer for 15 to 20 minutes or until potatoes are tender. Remove bay leaf and discard. Remove pan from heat and set aside to cool slightly.

4 Place soup in batches in a food processor or blender and process until smooth. Return soup to a clean saucepan, bring to the boil and simmer for 2 to 3 minutes or until soup is hot. Stir in chopped parsley and season to taste with black pepper.

Vegetable soup with pistou

1 Heat 1 tablespoon olive oil in a large saucepan over a medium heat, add onions, leeks and thyme and cook, stirring, for 5 minutes or until onions and leeks are soft.

2 Add celery, potatoes and carrots and cook, stirring, for 5 minutes. Add zucchini, green beans, canned beans and water and bring to the boil. Reduce heat and simmer for 30 minutes or until vegetables are tender. Season to taste with black pepper.

3 To make *pistou*, place basil, garlic, Parmesan cheese, olive oil and black pepper to taste in a food processor or blender and process to make a paste. Just prior to serving, stir *pistou* into soup.

Serves 6

1 tablespoon olive oil
2 onions, chopped
2 leeks, sliced
1 teaspoon chopped fresh thyme
3 stalks celery, sliced
2 large potatoes, diced
2 carrots, diced
2 zucchini, sliced
250g green beans, cut into 2.5cm pieces
440g canned lima, butter, red kidney or mixed beans, drained
8 cups water
freshly ground black pepper

Pistou

1 bunch basil, leaves removed and stems discarded
2 cloves garlic, chopped
125g Parmesan cheese, chopped
1/4 cup olive oil
freshly grouns black pepper

Oriental noodle soup

4 cups vegetable stock

½ cup tamari

250g bean thread noodles

375g tofu, roughly chopped

150g bok choy, chopped

1 stalk fresh lemongrass, chopped, or 1 teaspoon dried lemongrass or 1 teaspoon finely grated lemon rind

3 spring onions, sliced diagonally

5cm piece fresh ginger, sliced

200g straw or button mushrooms, chopped

1 tablespoon chopped fresh mint

2 tablespoons chopped fresh coriander

100g bean sprouts

Serves 4

1 Place stock and *tamari* in a large saucepan and bring to the boil. Reduce heat, add noodles, tofu, bok choy, lemongrass or lemon rind, spring onions, ginger, mushrooms, mint and coriander and simmer for 20 minutes.

2 To serve, divide bean sprouts between four warmed serving bowls and ladle over hot soup.

Note: Tamari is also called tamari shoyu or Japanese soy sauce. Made only from natural products, soya beans and salt, it contains no monosodium glutamate (MSG) which is often found in Chinese soy sauce. It is also lighter in flavour.

Carrot and orange soup

1 Heat oil in a large saucepan. Add leeks and cook over a medium heat, stirring, for 5 minutes or until golden.

2 Add carrots, curry powder, lemon rind and orange juice to pan, bring to the boil and simmer for 10 minutes or until carrots are soft.

3 Stir in coconut milk and stock and simmer for 10 minutes longer. Remove pan from heat and set aside to cool slightly. Place soup mixture, in batches, in a food processor or blender and process until smooth.

5 Return soup to a clean saucepan and heat over a medium heat, stirring, for 4 to 5 minutes or until hot. Season to taste with black pepper. Serve soup topped with yoghurt, cashew nuts and mint.

Note: If commercially made coconut milk is unavailable, you can make it using desiccated coconut and water. Place 500g desiccated coconut in a bowl and pour over 3 cups boiling water. Leave to stand for 30 minutes, then strain, squeezing the coconut to extract as much liquid as possible.

1 tablespoon vegetable oil

2 leeks, thinly sliced

6 large carrots, sliced

2 tablespoons curry powder

1 tablespoon finely grated lemon rind

1 cup orange juice

1 1/2 cups coconut milk

2 cups vegetable stock

freshly ground black pepper

1/3 cup natural yoghurt

100g cashew nuts, roasted and chopped

1 tablespoon chopped fresh mint

Serves 4

Farmhouse potato soup

2 large onions
2 cloves garlic
4 cups chicken stock
8 medium potatoes, peeled
2 bay leaves
2 cups milk
salt
pepper
2 tablespoons chopped parsley

Serves 4–6

1 Peel onions and chop finely. Crush, peel and chop garlic.

2 Sauté onion and garlic in a large saucepan for 5 minutes until onion is clear. Pour in chicken stock and bring to the boil. Cut potatoes into 2cm cubes. Add to stock with bay leaves.

3 Cover and simmer for 10 minutes or until potatoes are tender. Using a slotted spoon, remove about half the potato cubes and set aside. Mash soup with a potato masher.

4 Return potato cubes to soup. Add milk and bring to the boil. Season with salt and pepper. Mix parsley through.

Spiked pumpkin soup

1 Cut pumpkin into cubes. Peel onion and chop roughly. Crush and peel garlic. Peel carrot and slice. Trim celery and cut into cubes.

2 Melt butter in a large saucepan. Sauté onion, garlic, carrot and celery for 5 minutes.

3 Add chilli, ginger, cumin, coriander and cayenne and cook for 1 minute. Add bay leaves and stock. Bring to the boil. Add pumpkin and simmer for 20 minutes or until pumpkin is soft.

4 Remove bay leaves. Pour into a food processor or blender and process until smooth. Serve hot, garnished with parsley.

500g pumpkin, peeled and deseeded

1 onion

2 cloves garlic

1 carrot

1 stick celery

30g butter

1 tablespoon prepared chilli

$^1/_2$ teaspoon ground ginger

$^1/_2$ teaspoon ground cumin

$^1/_2$ teaspoon ground coriander

pinch cayenne pepper

2 bay leaves

6 cups chicken stock

chopped parsley

Serves 4–6

Virginia's asparagus soup

1kg asparagus

6 cups low-fat milk

2 vegetable stock cubes

30g butter

2 tablespoons flour

steamed asparagus spears, croutons or flaked almonds

Serves 4

1 Snap tough ends off asparagus. Place asparagus and milk in a saucepan. Crumble in stock cubes. Bring slowly to the boil. Simmer, uncovered, for 10 to 15 minutes until asparagus is just tender.

2 Process in a food processor or blender until chunky. Melt butter in a large saucepan. Add flour and cook until pale golden. Add soup and stir until it comes back to the boil.

3 Serve garnished with steamed asparagus spears, croutons or flaked almonds.

Quick mushroom soup

200g button mushrooms

2 cloves garlic

1 tablespoon butter

1 packet mushroom soup mix

1 cup water

1 cup low-fat milk

2 tablespoons chopped parsley

freshly ground black pepper

Serves 2–3

1 Wipe mushrooms and slice thinly. Crush, peel and finely chop garlic. Melt butter in a medium-sized saucepan.

2 Sauté mushrooms and garlic in butter for 2 to 3 minutes. Mix soup mix and water together. Pour into the saucepan and bring to the boil. Add milk. Bring to the boil. Reduce heat and simmer for 3 to 4 minutes.

3 Serve garnished with chopped parsley and freshly ground black pepper.

Curried lentil soup

2 tablespoons vegetable oil

1 onion, chopped

2 teaspoons curry powder

½ teaspoon ground cumin

1 tablespoon tomato paste

6 cups vegetable stock

125g red or green lentils

1 small head broccoli, broken into florets

2 carrots, chopped

1 parsnip, chopped

1 stalk celery, chopped

freshly ground black pepper

1 tablespoon chopped fresh parsley

Serves 6

1 Heat oil in a large saucepan. Add onion, curry powder and cumin and cook, stirring occasionally, for 4 to 5 minutes or until onion is soft. Stir in tomato paste and stock and bring to the boil. Reduce heat, add lentils, cover and simmer for 30 minutes.

2 Add broccoli, carrots, parsnip and celery and cook, covered, for 30 minutes longer or until vegetables are tender. Season to taste with black pepper. Just prior to serving, stir in parsley.

Note: This thick and hearty soup can be made ahead of time and makes a great main meal.

Winter vegetable soup

- 2 tablespoons vegetable oil
- 1 large onion, sliced
- 1 clove garlic, crushed
- 2 stalks celery, chopped
- 2 carrots, chopped
- 1 turnip, chopped
- 440g canned tomatoes, undrained and mashed
- 2 tablespoons tomato paste
- 1 tablespoon finely chopped fresh basil
- 1 teaspoon dried oregano
- 1 teaspoon sugar
- 6 cups vegetable stock
- 125g small pasta shells
- 315g canned red kidney beans, drained and rinsed
- freshly ground black pepper

Serves 6

1 Heat oil in a large saucepan. Add onion, garlic, celery, carrots and turnip and cook, stirring occasionally, for 4 to 5 minutes or until vegetables are just tender.

2 Stir in tomatoes, tomato paste, basil, oregano, sugar and stock and bring to the boil. Reduce heat and simmer for 30 to 45 minutes.

3 Stir in pasta and beans. Season to taste with black pepper and simmer, uncovered, for 30 minutes.

Note: A hearty meal in itself that will satisfy even the hungriest members of your family. Delicious sprinkled with freshly chopped parsley and Parmesan cheese and served with crusty bread.

Tomato salsa on bruschetta

Roasted garlic dressing

2 garlic cloves, unpeeled

2 tablespoons balsamic vinegar

1 tablespoon olive oil

Grilled tomato salsa

500g cherry tomatoes, halved

2 tablespoons olive oil

6 small bocconcini cheeses, chopped

4 tablespoons torn fresh basil leaves

crushed black peppercorns

12 slices crusty Italian bread

Makes 12

1 Preheat barbecue to a medium heat.

2 To make the dressing, place garlic cloves on barbecue plate (griddle) and cook for 1 to 2 minutes each side or until flesh is soft. Squeeze flesh from garlic cloves and mash. Place garlic, vinegar and oil in a screwtop jar and shake to combine.

3 To make salsa, combine tomatoes and oil in a bowl and toss to coat. Place tomatoes, cut side down, on barbecue plate and cook for 1 minute each side. Place tomatoes, cheese, basil and black peppercorns to taste in a bowl, add dressing and toss to combine.

4 Lightly brush bread with oil, place on barbecue grill and toast for 1 minute each side. To serve, pile tomato salsa onto bread and serve immediately.

Tapenade

125g pitted black olives

1 can anchovy fillets, drained

1 tablespoon capers, drained and rinsed

2 tablespoons olive oil

1 clove garlic, crushed

2 teaspoons lemon juice

3 tablespoons low-fat natural yoghurt

freshly ground black pepper

1 tablespoon chopped fresh basil

Makes ½ cup

1 Place olives, anchovies, capers, oil, garlic and lemon juice in a food processor or blender and process to make a paste.

2 Transfer paste to a small bowl, add yoghurt and black pepper to taste and mix to combine. Sprinkle with basil. Cover and refrigerate for 1 hour or until ready to serve.

Mushroom mix

- *350g mixed mushrooms*
- *3 spring onions*
- *1 clove garlic*
- *1 tablespoon sesame oil*
- *1 tablespoon finely chopped root ginger*
- *2 tablespoons water*
- *2 tablespoons soy sauce*
- *1 tablespoon chilli sauce*
- *1 tablespoon honey*

Serves 4–6

1 Prepare mushrooms depending on type, cutting into thick slices if large or leaving whole if small. Wash and trim spring onions. Cut into 1cm pieces on the diagonal.

2 Crush, peel and chop garlic. Heat oil in a wok or frying pan and stir-fry spring onions, garlic and ginger for 2 to 3 minutes. Add mushrooms and water and stir-fry for 1 minute.

3 Add soy and chilli sauces and honey and heat through. Serve immediately.

Pumpkin and *Pine nut* filo triangles

1 cup cold cooked mashed pumpkin

¼ cup chopped roasted pinenuts

¼ teaspoon ground nutmeg

1 tablespoon chopped fresh chives

12 sheets filo pastry

50g butter

Makes 12

1 Mix pumpkin, pine nuts, nutmeg and chives together. Place four sheets of filo under a damp tea-towel. Melt butter.

2 Brush butter between each layer of pastry. Divide pastry into four even-sized strips. Have strips running away from you. Place a tablespoon of pumpkin mixture at top right-hand corner of pastry strip. Fold left corner over to enclose filling. Fold pastry over and over to make a tight triangle. Repeat with remaining pastry. Brush with melted butter.

3 Bake at 200°C for 10 to 15 minutes or until golden.

Felafels

500g chickpeas
3 cloves garlic, crushed
1 small onion, chopped
4 spring onions, chopped
2 tablespoons chopped fresh coriander
2 tablespoons chopped fresh parsley
1 teaspoon ground cumin
1/2 teaspoon turmeric
vegetable oil, for deep frying

Serves 8

1 Place chickpeas in a large bowl, cover with cold water and set aside to soak overnight. Drain. Place chickpeas in large saucepan, cover with water and bring to the boil. Boil for 10 minutes, then reduce heat and simmer for 45 to 60 minutes or until chickpeas are tender. Drain and set aside to cool.

2 Place chickpeas, garlic, onion, spring onions, coriander, parsley, cumin and turmeric in a food processor or blender and combine.

3 Heat oil in a large saucepan until a cube of bread dropped in browns in 50 seconds. Shape tablespoons of chickpea mixture into balls and deep-fry, a few at a time, for 3 minutes or until golden brown. Drain on absorbent kitchen paper.

Note: To speed preparation, omit step 1 and use canned chickpeas. You will need two 440g cans and the chickpeas should be drained and rinsed before making the felafel.

Hot broccoli and cheese terrine

1 Boil, steam or microwave broccoli until tender. Drain and set aside. Melt butter in a frying pan. Add onion and cook until soft and transparent.

2 Puree broccoli, onion, egg yolks, parsley, chives and cottage cheese in a food processor or blender. Transfer to a bowl and mix in breadcrumbs, Parmesan and tasty cheese. Season with pepper. Beat egg whites until stiff and fold through the broccoli mixture.

3 Spoon mixture into a greased and lined 21 x 14cm loaf pan. Bake at 200°C for 25 minutes or until set. Cool for 5 minutes before turning out. Cut into slices to serve.

Note: This delicious combination makes a perfect entrée when served with a fresh tomato sauce.

500g broccoli, cut into florets

15g butter

1 large onion, finely chopped

2 eggs, separated

1 tablespoon chopped fresh parsley

1 tablespoon chopped fresh chives

250g cottage cheese

3 slices multigrain bread, crumbed

3 tablespoons grated Parmesan cheese

3 tablespoons grated tasty cheese

freshly ground black pepper

Serves 6

Parsnip fritters

- *3 large parsnips, peeled and sliced*
- *15g butter*
- *2 tablespoons plain flour*
- *1 teaspoon baking powder*
- *2 tablespoons finely chopped fresh parsley*
- *2 tablespoons finely chopped fresh chives*
- *2 tablespoons finely chopped fresh dill*
- *2 eggs*
- *1/2 cup polyunsaturated oil*

Serves 6

1 Boil, steam or microwave parsnips until tender. Drain and mash with butter.

2 Using a wooden spoon, beat in flour, baking powder, parsley, chives, dill and eggs.

3 Heat oil in a frying pan. Drop tablespoons of parsnip batter into oil and cook until golden and puffed. Drain on paper towel.

Note: These easy herb-flavoured parsnip fritters are delicious with salad for lunch.

Puff mushroom pizza

375g prepared puff pastry

60g grated Parmesan cheese

125g grated mozzarella cheese

1 onion, thinly sliced

200g mushrooms, sliced

3 tomatoes, cut into 1 cm slices

10 pitted black olives

2 teaspoons chopped fresh oregano or 1/2 teaspoon dried oregano

2 teaspoons chopped fresh thyme or 1/2 teaspoon dried thyme

Serves 6

1 Roll out pastry to fit a greased 26 x 32cm Swiss roll tin.

2 Sprinkle pastry with Parmesan and mozzarella cheese, then top with onion, mushrooms, tomatoes and olives. Sprinkle with oregano and thyme and bake for 30 minutes or until pastry is puffed and golden. Serve hot, warm or cold.

Note: This quick pastry-based pizza is great for weekend meals and leftovers are ideal for packed lunches.

Wrapped asparagus

18 asparagus spears

2 teaspoons wasabi powder

2 teaspoons water

1 teaspoon sugar

¼ teaspoon ground chilli

6 wonton wrappers

1 teaspoon sesame oil

Makes 12

1 Snap tough ends from asparagus and cut spears in half. Cook in a frying pan of boiling salted water for 3 minutes. Drain.

2 Mix wasabi powder, water, sugar and chilli together in a small bowl. Spread wasabi mixture onto wonton wrappers.

3 Wrap a wonton wrapper around three asparagus spears. Repeat with remaining wrappers and spears. Place seam side down on an oven tray. Brush with oil.

4 Grill for 1 minute each side or until lightly golden. Cut in half to serve. Serve immediately.

Zucchini and carrot terrine

1 Wash and trim zucchini. Cut into chunks. Trim carrots, scrub or peel and cut into pieces. Steam or microwave carrots and zucchini until tender. Cool.

2 Press juice from zucchini by pressing them with a saucer in a sieve. Puree zucchini in a food processor or blender. Add two eggs, quarter of a cup of cream and curry powder to puree and mix in. Spread mixture into a baking-paper-lined 16 x 9cm loaf tin.

3 Wash spinach and remove stems. Blanch in boiling water for 2 minutes. Drain. Lay spinach over zucchini. Puree carrots in a food processor or blender. Mix in remaining eggs, cream and nutmeg. Spread over spinach.

4 Cover loaf tin with oiled foil and place in a roasting dish. Place roasting dish in oven and pour water around terrine to come halfway up sides of tin. Bake at 180°C for 1 1/4 hours or until an inserted skewer comes out clean. Remove from water bath and stand for 10 minutes before turning out. Serve warm, cut into slices and accompanied by French bread.

4 medium zucchini

3 medium carrots

4 eggs

1/2 cup cream

1/4 teaspoon curry powder

250g spinach

pinch grated nutmeg

salt

pepper

Serves 4

Goat's cheese and polenta pizza

Polenta base

100g self-raising flour

155g corn meal (polenta)

2 eggs, lightly beaten

$^{3}/_{4}$ cup milk

1 tablespoon olive oil

Red capsicum topping

3 tablespoons tomato paste

2 red capsicum, roasted and skins removed

125g button mushrooms, sliced

125g marinated eggplant

125g goat's cheese, crumbled or chopped

1 tablespoon fresh oregano or $^{1}/_{2}$ teaspoon dried oregano

freshly ground black pepper

Serves 4

1 To make base, place flour and polenta in a bowl. Make a well in the centre and stir in eggs and milk to form a smooth batter.

2 Heat oil in a 25cm heavy-based frying pan over a medium heat. Pour in batter and cook for 5 minutes. Carefully turn base over in pan and cook for 5 minutes longer. Remove pan from heat.

3 For topping, spread base with tomato paste and top with red capsicum, mushrooms, eggplant, goat's cheese, oregano and black pepper to taste.

4 Place pizza in pan under a preheated hot grill and cook for 3 minutes or until topping is hot. Serve hot or cold, cut into wedges.

Watercress and stilton pizza

6 small pita bread rounds

1 bunch watercress, broken into sprigs

3 pears, cored, peeled and sliced

200g Stilton or other blue cheese, sliced

freshly ground black pepper

Serves 6

1 Toast pita bread rounds under a preheated medium grill for 2 to 3 minutes each side or until crisp.

2 Top each pita bread round with watercress, pears, cheese and black pepper to taste.

3 Return to grill and cook for 1 minute or until cheese melts and pears are warm.

Mediterranean rocket salad

100g rocket

1 bunch curly endive, leaves separated

1 red onion, thinly sliced

440g canned chickpeas, drained

4 roma tomatoes, quartered

125g feta cheese, roughly chopped

250g black olives

8 marinated artichoke hearts, halved

4 tablespoons pine nuts, toasted

balsamic or red wine vinegar

freshly ground black pepper

Serves 4

1 Arrange rocket, endive, onion, chickpeas, tomatoes, feta cheese, olives, artichokes and pine nuts on a large serving platter.

2 Drizzle balsamic or red wine vinegar over salad and season with black pepper. Cover and refrigerate salad until required.

Note: If canned chickpeas are unavailable, use cold cooked chickpeas instead.

Watercress and orange salad

1 Place burghul in a bowl, cover with boiling water and allow to stand for 10 to 15 minutes or until soft. Drain.

2 Place burghul, watercress, avocado, oranges, tomatoes and red capsicum in a salad bowl.

3 To make dressing, place orange juice, poppy seeds and vinegar in a screwtop jar and shake well to combine. Spoon dressing over salad and toss. Cover and refrigerate until required.

1 cup burghul (cracker wheat)

2 cups boiling water

1 bunch watercress, broken into sprigs

1 avocado, stoned, peeled and chopped

2 oranges, white pith removed, flesh chopped

250g cherry tomatoes, halved

1 red capsicum, diced

Orange dressing

½ cup orange juice

1 tablespoon poppy seeds

2 tablespoons red wine vinegar

Serves 4

Caesar salad

4 cloves garlic

$\frac{1}{2}$ cup olive oil

3 cups baguette cubes

1 or 2 cos lettuces

$\frac{1}{2}$ teaspoon salt

3 tablespoons lemon juice

$\frac{1}{2}$ teaspoon Worcestershire sauce

3 lightly hard-boiled eggs

$\frac{1}{2}$ cup grated or shaved Parmesan cheese

1 can anchovy fillets

Serves 4–6

1 Crush and peel garlic. Mash two cloves of garlic and mix with quarter of a cup of olive oil. Mix well so garlic flavours oil.

2 Brush oil over bread cubes. Place bread on baking tray and bake at 180°C for 10 to 15 minutes or until golden, turning occasionally.

3 Wash and dry lettuce. Tear leaves into pieces and place in a bowl. Mash remaining garlic with salt. Mix garlic, lemon juice, remaining olive oil and Worcestershire sauce together. Pour over lettuce.

4 Shell eggs, chop roughly and add to salad. Sprinkle Parmesan cheese over and toss to mix. Cut anchovies into pieces and place on top of salad with croutons.

Note: For soft-boiled eggs, cook for 5 minutes.

Greek salad

6 medium tomatoes
250g feta cheese
1 cup black olives
½ cup basil leaves
3 tablespoons olive oil
freshly ground black pepper

Serves 4–6

1 Cut stem end from tomatoes and discard. Slice tomatoes thickly and arrange on a serving platter. Crumble feta over tomatoes and arrange olives over.

2 Break basil leaves into pieces and scatter over tomatoes. Drizzle oil over tomatoes and coarsely grind black pepper over.

Note: If feta cheese isn't to your taste, replace with mounds of plain cottage cheese.

Eggplant salad

1 large eggplant

salt

1/4 cup oil

1 tablespoon chopped parsley

Dressing

1/4 cup red or white wine vinegar

1/4 cup extra virgin olive oil

1/4 teaspoon dried oregano

salt

freshly ground black pepper

Serves 4

1 Cut eggplant into 1cm-thick slices. Sprinkle with salt and leave for 30 minutes. Wash and pat dry. Heat oil in a frying pan and cook eggplant until lightly golden on each side. Arrange in a serving dish.

2 To make the dressing, place vinegar, oil, oregano, salt and pepper in a screwtop jar. Shake to combine. Pour dressing over and leave to marinate for at least 30 minutes before serving. Sprinkle with chopped parsley.

Note: Salting eggplant before cooking takes away the bitter flavours.

Beetroot salad

2 medium beetroots

2 Granny Smith apples

1 spring onion

¼ cup unsweetened natural yoghurt

1 tablespoon lemon juice

½ cup chopped parsley

Serves 6

1 Trim, peel and grate beetroot. Grate apple, leaving skin on. Place grated apple in a sieve and drain. Trim spring onion and slice thinly.

2 Mix beetroot, apple and spring onion together. Fold yoghurt and lemon juice through. Mix in parsley.

Raw mushroom salad

500g button mushrooms, thinly sliced

1 tablespoon finely chopped fresh chives

1 tablespoon finely chopped fresh parsley

½ red capsicum, diced

Marinade

½ cup olive oil

3 tablespoons lemon juice

1 tablespoon white wine vinegar

1 clove garlic, crushed

¼ teaspoon chilli powder

Serves 6

1 Place mushrooms in a bowl. To make marinade, combine oil, lemon juice, vinegar, garlic and chilli powder in a screwtop jar. Shake well and pour over mushrooms. Toss and leave to marinate for 2 to 3 hours, tossing from time to time.

2 Gently fold through chives, parsley and capsicum and serve.

Note: An all-time favourite, this mushroom salad is easy to make and delicious served as part of a salad buffet or with a barbecue.

Minestrone salad

1 Cook pasta in boiling water in a large saucepan following packet directions. Drain, rinse under cold running water and set aside to cool completely.

2 Place chickpeas, carrots, zucchini, celery, red capsicum, beans, tomatoes and pasta in a bowl and toss to combine.

3 Arrange lettuce on a serving platter and top with pasta mixture.

4 To make dressing, place pesto, yoghurt and mayonnaise in a bowl and mix to combine. Drizzle over salad and serve.

250g pasta shells

440g canned chickpeas, rinsed and drained

2 carrots, diced

2 zucchini, diced

2 stalks celery, diced

1 red capsicum, diced

155g green beans, blanched

3 plum tomatoes, cut into wedges

250g mixed lettuce leaves

Pesto dressing

125g ready-made pesto of choice

1/2 cup natural yoghurt

2 tablespoons mayonnaise

Serves 4

Endive and goat's cheese salad

- *8 thick slices goat's cheese*
- *1 tablespoon olive oil*
- *freshly ground black pepper*
- *300g curly endive leaves*
- *250g cherry tomatoes, halved*
- *1 cucumber, sliced*
- *1 small baguette, sliced and toasted*
- *2 tablespoons white wine vinegar*

Serves 6

1 Brush goat's cheese with oil and season with black pepper. Place under a preheated medium grill and cook for 3 minutes each side or until golden.

2 Arrange endive leaves, tomatoes, cucumber, toast and goat's cheese on a serving platter. Drizzle with vinegar and serve immediately.

Note: A simple yet delicious salad with a strong Mediterranean influence. Curly endive is a member of the chicory family and has a more bitter taste than lettuce.

Nashi and nut salad

300g assorted lettuce leaves

2 nashi pears, cored and sliced

2 peaches, sliced

125g macadamia or brazil nuts

2 tablespoons sesame seeds, toasted

Chilli-sesame dressing

2 teaspoons sesame oil

1 tablespoon vegetable oil

1 tablespoon sweet chilli sauce

2 tablespoons lemon juice

Serves 4

1 Arrange lettuce leaves, nashi pears, peaches, macadamia or brazil nuts and sesame seeds on a large serving platter.

2 To make dressing, place sesame and vegetable oils, chilli sauce and lemon juice in a screwtop jar and shake well to combine. Spoon dressing over salad and toss. Cover and refrigerate salad until required.

Note: Native to Australia, the macadamia nut has a very hard shell and a delicious rich buttery flavour. In most recipes that call for macadamia nuts, brazil nuts can be used instead. The nashi pear is also known as the Chinese pear and is originally from northern Asia. If nashis are unavailable, pears or apples are a delicious alternative for this salad.

Marinated tofu salad

4 tablespoons soy sauce

2 teaspoons vegetable oil

½ teaspoon finely chopped fresh ginger

1 tablespoon lemon juice

2 teaspoons dry white wine

500g tofu, cut into cubes

1 lettuce, leaves separated

2 tomatoes, cut into wedges

60g snow pea sprouts or watercress

2 carrots, sliced

1 tablespoon sesame seeds, toasted

Serves 4

1 Place soy sauce, oil, ginger, lemon juice and wine in a small bowl. Add tofu and toss to coat. Cover and set aside to marinate for 10 to 15 minutes.

2 Place lettuce, tomatoes, snow pea sprouts or watercress and carrots in a bowl. Drain tofu and reserve marinade. Add tofu to salad, toss to combine and sprinkle with sesame seeds. Just prior to serving, drizzle with reserved marinade.

Note: An easy summer dish, this salad requires only wholegrain or rye bread to make it a complete meal.

Mexican salad

1 avocado, stoned, peeled and chopped

1 tablespoon lime or lemon juice

lettuce leaves of your choice

2 tomatoes, cut into wedges

1 green capsicum, chopped

315g canned red kidney beans, drained

2 teaspoons chopped fresh coriander

freshly ground black pepper

Serves 2

1 Place avocado and lime or lemon juice in a small bowl and toss to coat.

2 Arrange lettuce leaves, tomatoes, green capsicum, beans and avocado mixture attractively in two lunch boxes. Sprinkle with coriander and season to taste with black pepper. Cover and refrigerate until required.

Note: Tossing the avocado in lime or lemon juice helps prevent it from discolouring.

Salad of roast tomatoes

6 plum tomatoes, halved

8 cloves garlic, peeled

freshly ground black pepper

2 tablespoons olive oil

350g assorted lettuce leaves

185g feta cheese, crumbled

1 yellow or red capsicum, sliced

Tangy dressing

3 tablespoons balsamic or red wine vinegar

3 tablespoons tomato puree

3 drops Tabasco sauce

Serves 4

1 Place tomatoes and garlic on a baking tray, sprinkle with black pepper to taste and oil and bake for 30 minutes or until tomatoes are soft and golden. Set aside to cool completely.

2 Arrange lettuce leaves, feta cheese, capsicum, tomatoes and garlic attractively on serving plates.

3 To make dressing, place vinegar, tomato puree, Tabasco and black pepper to taste in a screwtop jar and shake well to combine. Drizzle dressing over salad and serve immediately.

Note: The sweet rich flavour of roast tomatoes is a perfect partner for the creamy piquant feta cheese in this salad.

Crunchy snow pea salad

200g prepared snow peas

1 mignonette lettuce

200g mixed bean sprouts

1 tomato peeled, seeded and cut into strips

Dressing

3 tablespoons vegetable oil

$\frac{1}{2}$ teaspoon sesame oil

1 tablespoon soy sauce

1 tablespoon cider vinegar

1 teaspoon grated fresh ginger

freshly ground black pepper

Serves 4

1 Blanch snow peas in boiling water and refresh under cold running water then drain.

2 Line a salad bowl with lettuce. Arrange snow peas, bean sprouts and tomato strips over lettuce.

3 To make dressing, place vegetable oil, sesame oil, soy, vinegar, ginger and pepper in a screwtop jar. Shake well to combine and pour over salad.

Note: Choose a variety of bean sprouts to give added flavour and texture to the salad. You might like to use alfalfa, mung bean sprouts or snow pea sprouts.

Barbecued *potato salad*

6 large potatoes

¼ cup garlic-flavoured olive oil

½ cup mayonnaise

½ cup sour cream

2 tablespoons basil pesto

½ cup pitted black olives

fresh basil leaves

Serves 4–6

1 Scrub potatoes and cook in boiling salted water for 10 minutes to partially cook. Drain. Cut into 2cm cubes and pour oil over them. Leave to marinate in oil for several hours if possible or until ready to cook.

2 Grill potatoes over a barbecue or under a hot grill, turning until golden brown, crisp and cooked.

3 Mix mayonnaise, sour cream and pesto together in a serving bowl. Toss potatoes in mayonnaise mixture with olives. Clean edges of bowl with a paper towel. Garnish with fresh basil.

Peperonata

400g canned tomatoes in juice

6 mixed capsicums – red, green and yellow

1 onion

1 clove garlic

2 tablespoons light olive oil

1 ½ tablespoons dried oregano

½ teaspoon dried basil

freshly ground black pepper

Serves 4

1 Chop tomatoes, removing cores. Cut capsicums in half lengthwise and remove seeds and cores. Slice flesh lengthwise.

2 Peel onion and slice. Crush, peel and chop garlic. Heat oil in a large frying pan. Add onion and garlic and sauté until clear. Add sliced capsicum and cook for 3 minutes.

3 Add tomatoes, oregano, basil and pepper. Cover and cook over a low heat for 15 minutes, stirring from time to time.

Tagliarini with pistachios

500g fresh spinach tagliarini

45g butter

60g pistachio nuts, shelled

4 tablespoons shredded fresh basil leaves

250g cherry tomatoes, halved

1 tablespoon green peppercorns in brine, drained

Serves 4

1 Cook tagliarini in boiling water in a large saucepan following packet directions. Drain, set aside and keep warm.

2 Melt butter in a frying pan, add pistachio nuts, basil, tomatoes and green peppercorns. Cook over a medium heat, stirring constantly, for 4 to 5 minutes or until heated through. Toss tomato mixture with pasta.

Note: Tagliarini is a flat ribbon pasta similar to tagliatelle but slightly narrower in width. If unavailable this dish is also delicious made with tagliatelle, fettuccine or spaghetti.

Chilli pasta bake

1 Cook pasta in boiling water in a large saucepan following packet directions. Drain, stir in sour cream and spread over base of an ovenproof dish.

2 To make sauce, heat oil in a large saucepan. Add onions and cook over a medium heat, stirring, for 3 minutes or until onions are soft. Add cumin, coriander and chilli powder and cook, stirring constantly, for 1 minute longer. Stir in beans and tomato puree, bring to the boil and simmer for 5 minutes.

3 Pour sauce over pasta, sprinkle with cheese and bake for 15 to 20 minutes or until cheese melts and turns golden.

Note: Serve this tasty bake with steamed vegetables and cheese and basil bread.

375g penne pasta

300g sour cream

125g tasty cheese (mature Cheddar), grated

Chilli sauce

2 teaspoons vegetable oil

2 onions, chopped

1 teaspoon ground cumin

1 teaspoon ground coriander

1/2 teaspoon chilli powder

440g canned red kidney beans, drained

440g canned tomato puree

Serves 4

Hearty bean casserole

- *150g dried red kidney beans*
- *150g dried black-eyed beans*
- *1 tablespoon vegetable oil*
- *2 cloves garlic, crushed*
- *1 red onion, chopped*
- *440g canned peeled tomatoes, undrained and mashed*
- *1 tablespoon ground cumin*
- *1 tablespoon dry mustard*
- *2 tablespoons golden syrup*
- *1 tablespoon tomato paste*
- *2 carrots, thickly sliced*
- *3 zucchini, thickly sliced*
- *440g canned butter beans, rinsed and drained*
- *100g shelled fresh or frozen broad beans*
- *2 tablespoons chopped fresh oregano or 1 teaspoon dried oregano*

Serves 4

1 Place red kidney and black-eyed beans in a large bowl, cover with water and set aside to soak overnight. Drain. Bring a large saucepan of water to the boil, add beans and boil for 10 minutes. Reduce heat and simmer for 1 hour or until beans are tender. Drain and set aside.

2 Heat oil in a large saucepan over a medium heat, add garlic and onion and cook, stirring, for 3 minutes or until onion is soft and golden. Add tomatoes, cumin, mustard, golden syrup and tomato paste and bring to the boil. Reduce heat and simmer for 5 minutes.

3 Add cooked beans, carrots, zucchini, butter beans, broad beans and oregano to pan and simmer for 30 minutes or until vegetables are tender.

Note: All types of beans adapt to a huge range of seasonings. The beans in this casserole can be varied to accommodate whatever you have available. As an alternative, try a combination of haricot and butter beans with chickpeas, and substitute your favourite spices or dried herbs for the ground cumin and oregano.

Okra and bean stew

1 Heat oil in a large saucepan. Add garlic, chillies and onions and cook over a medium heat, stirring constantly, for 5 minutes or until onions are soft and golden.

2 Add okra, eggplant, tomatoes, beans, tofu, wine and sugar. Bring to the boil, then reduce heat and simmer for 30 minutes. Stir in basil and black pepper to taste.

Note: Serve this tasty vegetable stew with wholemeal pasta or brown rice. When preparing fresh okra, wash it well and handle it carefully. Rub it gently under running water to remove the fuzzy outer layer.

- *2 teaspoons vegetable oil*
- *2 cloves garlic, crushed*
- *2 fresh red chillies, chopped*
- *2 onions, sliced*
- *250g okra*
- *2 eggplants, chopped*
- *2 x 440g canned peeled tomatoes, undrained and mashed*
- *440g canned red kidney beans, rinsed*
- *250g firm tofu, cut into chunks*
- *½ cup red wine*
- *1 tablespoon brown sugar*
- *3 tablespoons chopped fresh basil*
- *freshly ground black pepper*

Serves 4

Beans with chilli

3 tablespoons water

2 onions, chopped

2 cloves garlic, crushed

1 red capsicum, chopped

2 x 440g canned red kidney beans, drained

2 carrots, diced

250g green beans, cut into 2.5cm pieces

2 x 440g canned tomatoes, undrained and mashed

1 cup tomato juice

1/4 teaspoon chilli powder, or according to taste

4 tablespoons chopped fresh parsley

Serves 6

1 Heat water in a saucepan, add onion and garlic and cook, stirring, for 3 to 4 minutes or until onion is soft.

2 Add red capsicum, red kidney beans, carrots, green beans, tomatoes, tomato juice and chilli powder and bring to the boil. Reduce heat and simmer, stirring occasionally, for 15 to 20 minutes or until mixture reduces and thickens. Stir in parsley and serve.

Note: For a complete meal, accompany with rice, pasta or crusty bread and a tossed green salad.

Capsicum filled with beans

1 Cut capsicums in half lengthwise and remove seeds and pith. Place capsicum shells on a lightly greased baking tray and set aside.

2 Heat oil in a large saucepan, add onion and cook, stirring, for 2 to 3 minutes or until onion is soft.

3 Add cumin, garlic, tomato paste, stock, tomatoes and red kidney beans to pan and bring to the boil. Reduce heat and simmer, uncovered, for 10 minutes or until mixture reduces and thickens. Season to taste with black pepper.

4 Spoon filling into prepared capsicum shells and bake for 20 minutes or until capsicums are tender.

Note: This tasty combination of red kidney beans and tomato is also delicious served on its own, or you might like to try it as a filling for baby pumpkins.

4 red or green capsicums

Bean filling

2 tablespoons olive oil

1 onion, chopped

2 tablespoons ground cumin

1 clove garlic, crushed

3 tablespoons tomato paste

1/2 cup vegetable stock

440g canned tomatoes, undrained and mashed

440g canned red kidney beans, drained

freshly ground black pepper

Serves 4

Spinach and basil risotto

500g spinach, stalks removed and leaves chopped

1 cup water

60g butter

1 large onion, finely chopped

2 cloves garlic, crushed

2 cups brown rice

½ cup white wine

5 cups hot vegetable stock

30g fresh basil leaves

2 tablespoons olive oil

4 tablespoons pine nuts, toasted

Serves 4

1 Place spinach and water in a saucepan, bring to the boil and cook for 1 minute or until spinach is tender. Remove from heat and set aside to cool.

2 Place spinach mixture in a food processor or blender and process until smooth. Set aside.

3 Melt butter in a saucepan, add onion and garlic and cook for 4 to 5 minutes or until onion is soft. Add rice to pan and stir to coat with butter mixture. Pour in wine and half the stock. Cook over a medium heat, stirring occasionally, until almost all the liquid is absorbed. Stir in remaining stock with reserved spinach mixture and cook until almost all the liquid is absorbed.

4 Place basil, oil and 3 tablespoons pine nuts in food processor or blender and process until smooth. Stir into rice mixture. Sprinkle with remaining pine nuts and serve immediately.

Note: Risotto is an Italian favourite. Wonderful as a first course, main course or an accompaniment to meat, fish or poultry, it is nutritious and easy to make.

Wholemeal spinach quiche

1 Roll out pastry and line the base and sides of a lightly greased 23cm flan tin. Trim edges of pastry and line base with baking paper. Fill with uncooked rice and bake for 15 minutes at 220°C. Remove rice and paper and bake for 10 minutes longer. Remove from oven and set aside to cool slightly.

2 To make filling, melt butter in a frying pan, add onion and cook over a medium heat for 4 to 5 minutes or until soft. Stir in spinach and cook for 2 to 3 minutes longer or until spinach wilts. Remove pan from heat and set aside.

3 Place eggs, sour cream, cheese, nutmeg and black pepper to taste in a bowl and mix to combine. Spread spinach mixture over base of pastry case, then carefully spoon in egg mixture. Reduce oven temperature to 180°C and bake for 30 minutes or until filling is firm.

Note: When making pastry, have all the utensils and ingredients as cold as possible. In hot weather, chill the utensils before using. Wash your hands in cold water and use only your fingertips for kneading.

150g prepared wholemeal pastry

Spinach filling

30g butter

1 onion, finely chopped

½ bunch spinach, stalks removed and leaves finely shredded

3 eggs, lightly beaten

300g sour cream

60g grated tasty cheese (mature Cheddar)

pinch ground nutmeg

freshly ground black pepper

Serves 4

Vegetable chilli

1 large eggplant, cut into 1cm cubes

salt

4 tablespoons olive oil

1 large onion, chopped

1 clove garlic, crushed

1 green capsicum, sliced

425g canned peeled tomatoes

2 zucchini, sliced

1 teaspoon hot chilli powder

½ teaspoon ground cumin

4 sprigs fresh parsley, finely chopped

500g canned three-bean mix

freshly ground black pepper

Serves 6

1 Sprinkle eggplant with salt. Stand for 15 to 20 minutes. Rinse under cold water and pat dry with absorbent paper.

2 Heat oil in a large frying pan and cook eggplant until just tender. Add more oil if necessary. Transfer eggplant to a large casserole dish.

3 Add onion, garlic and capsicum to pan and cook until onion softens. Stir in tomatoes, zucchini, chilli powder, cumin, parsley, beans and pepper to taste. Cook until heated through. Spoon into dish with eggplant.

4 Bake at 180°C for 1½ hours or until eggplant skin is tender and the casserole is bubbling hot.

Savoury pumpkin flan

4 sheets filo pastry

2 tablespoons vegetable oil

1 onion, chopped

250g pumpkin or carrots, cooked and mashed

200g grated tasty cheese (mature Cheddar)

2 eggs, separated

2 tablespoons sour cream or natural yoghurt

pinch chilli powder

freshly ground black pepper

1 tablespoon chopped fresh parsley

Serves 4

1 Brush each sheet of pastry with oil and fold in half. Layer pastry, one folded piece on top of the other to give eight layers. Place an 18cm flan dish upside down on layered pastry and cut around dish, making a circle 3cm larger. Lift all layers of pastry into dish and roll edges.

2 Cook onion in a frying pan for 4 to 5 minutes or until onion is opaque and soft. Place pumpkin or carrots, cheese, egg yolks, sour cream or yoghurt, chilli powder and black pepper to taste in a bowl and mix to combine.

3 Place egg whites in a bowl and beat until stiff peaks form. Fold egg white mixture into pumpkin mixture and spoon into pastry case. Sprinkle pumpkin mixture with parsley and bake at 200°C for 30 minutes or until pastry is golden and cooked.

Note: When incorporating beaten egg whites into a mixture, first stir in 1 tablespoon of beaten egg white, then lightly fold remaining beaten egg white through, working as quickly as possible.

Mushroom risotto

45g butter

200g flat mushrooms, thickly sliced

125g button mushrooms, halved

200g shiitake mushrooms

200g oyster mushrooms

2 cups arborio or risotto rice

4 cups hot vegetable stock

4 tablespoons grated Parmesan cheese

freshly ground black pepper

Serves 4

1 Melt 15g butter in a frying pan. Add flat, button, shiitake and oyster mushrooms and cook over a medium heat, stirring constantly, for 4 to 5 minutes or until mushrooms are soft. Remove pan from heat and set aside.

2 Melt remaining butter in a clean frying pan. Add rice and cook over a medium heat, stirring constantly, for 2 minutes. Pour 1 cup hot stock into rice and cook over a medium heat, stirring constantly, until stock is absorbed. Continue cooking in this way until all the stock is used and rice is tender.

3 Stir mushroom mixture, Parmesan cheese and black pepper to taste into rice mixture and cook for 2 minutes longer.

Note: Arborio or risotto rice is traditionally used for making risotto. It absorbs liquid without becoming soft and it is this special quality that makes it so suitable for risottos. If Arborio rice is unavailable, substitute short-grain rice. A risotto made in the traditional way, where liquid is added a little at a time as the rice cooks, will take 20 to 30 minutes to cook.

Tomato risotto

- *4 cups vegetable stock*
- *2 cups tomato juice*
- *15g butter*
- *600g arborio or risotto rice*
- *10 sun-dried tomatoes, sliced*
- *2 tomatoes, chopped*
- *125g pitted olives*
- *freshly ground black pepper*

Serves 6

1 Place stock and tomato juice in a large saucepan and bring to the boil over a medium heat. Reduce heat and keep warm.

2 Melt butter in a large saucepan. Add rice and cook over a medium heat, stirring constantly, for 2 minutes. Pour 1 cup stock mixture into rice and cook over a medium heat, stirring constantly, until stock is absorbed. Continue cooking in this way until all the stock is used and rice is tender.

3 Stir sun-dried tomatoes, tomatoes, olives and black pepper to taste into rice mixture and cook for 2 minutes longer.

Note: When serving a risotto, start with a salad and crusty bread and finish with fresh fruit or a dessert.

Spinach risotto with raisins and almonds

1 bunch English spinach

2 tablespoons oil

½ bunch shallots, chopped

¾ cup arborio rice

4 cups hot water

salt and freshly ground black pepper

3 tablespoons lemon juice

¾ cup raisins

60g almonds, blanched

Serves 3

1 Wash spinach, rinse and chop roughly. Heat oil in saucepan, add shallots and sauté a little. Add rice and stir until coated with oil and rice has coloured slightly, about 30 seconds.

2 Add spinach, hot water, salt, pepper and lemon juice. Cover and cook on medium heat for 10 minutes. Remove lid, stir to combine, add raisins, re-cover and cook 5 minutes more. Turn off heat and stand, covered, 5 minutes before serving to plump the rice. Sprinkle with almonds.

Spinach rice parcels

1 Boil, steam or microwave spinach leaves until wilted. Drain and pat dry with absorbent kitchen paper.

2 To make filling, place rice, wild rice, spring onions, avocado, orange rind, sultanas, tomatoes and black pepper to taste in a bowl and mix to combine.

3 Divide rice mixture between spinach leaves. Fold in sides of leaves and roll up to form a parcel.

4 Arrange spinach parcels side by side in a shallow ovenproof dish. Pour over stock, cover and bake for 15 minutes or until heated through.

8 spinach leaves, stalks removed

1 cup vegetable stock

Rice filling

1 cup rice, cooked

1 cup wild rice, cooked

2 spring onions, chopped

1 avocado, stoned, peeled and chopped

1 tablespoon finely grated orange rind

3 tablespoons sultanas

2 tomatoes, finely chopped

freshly ground black pepper

Serves 4

Garlic rice with currants and pinenuts

- 2 tablespoons olive oil
- 1 large onion, chopped
- 3–4 cloves garlic, finely chopped
- 1 ½ cups long grain rice
- ¼ cup pine nuts
- 400g can tomatoes, chopped, juice reserved
- ½ teaspoon sugar
- 1 teaspoon salt
- ¼ teaspoon black pepper
- 1 cup hot water
- ½ cup currants
- 2 tablespoons chopped parsley
- 2 tablespoons chopped mint

Serves 4

1 Heat oil in a large saucepan and gently fry onion until pale golden. Add garlic and stir to cook a little. Add rice and pine nuts and stir to coat grains with oil.

2 Add chopped tomatoes plus juice from can. Season with sugar, salt and pepper, and add hot water

3 Stir in all remaining ingredients and bring to the boil. Turn down heat and cook at a medium boil for 14 minutes, stirring occasionally during cooking. Turn off heat, cover tightly and stand 5 minutes before serving.

Mushroom gougère

1 To make pastry, place water and butter in a saucepan, cover and cook until butter melts and mixture just boils. Remove pan from heat and add flour. Stir vigorously with a wooden spoon over a low heat until mixture forms a ball and pulls away from sides of pan. Set aside to cool slightly.

2 Add eggs to pastry mixture one at a time, beating well after each addition until mixture is smooth and glossy. Spread mixture around sides of a greased shallow 23cm ovenproof dish.

3 To make filling, place mushrooms, eggs, sour cream, cream, flour, cheese, parsley, nutmeg and black pepper to taste in a bowl and mix to combine. Spoon filling into centre of pastry and bake for 35 to 40 minutes or until filling is firm and pastry is puffed and golden.

Note: Mushrooms should be stored in a brown paper bag or a cloth bag in the refrigerator. Stored in this way they will keep fresh for five to seven days. Never store mushrooms in a plastic bag as this causes them to sweat and deteriorate very quickly.

Choux pastry

1 cup water

90g butter

1 cup flour, sifted

4 eggs

Mushroom filling

155g button mushrooms, sliced

3 eggs, lightly beaten

155g sour cream

1/2 cup thickened (double) cream

1 tablespoon flour

125g grated tasty cheese (mature Cheddar)

1 tablespoon chopped fresh parsley

pinch ground nutmeg

freshly ground black pepper

Serves 4

Pasta with spinach mint sauce

500g fresh or dried spaghetti or bucatini

Spinach and mint sauce

500g frozen spinach, thawed and drained

250g feta cheese, crumbled

1 cup natural yoghurt

3 tablespoons chopped fresh mint

1 teaspoon finely grated lemon rind

Serves 4

1 Cook pasta in boiling water in a large saucepan following packet directions. Drain, set aside and keep warm.

2 To make sauce, place spinach, feta cheese, yoghurt, mint and lemon rind in the pan in which the pasta was cooked and cook over a low heat, stirring, for 2 minutes or until heated through.

3 Return pasta to pan and toss to combine. Cook over a low heat, stirring, for 2 minutes longer or until mixture is hot. Serve immediately.

Vegetable cannelloni

1 To make filling, heat oil in a frying pan over a medium heat. Add garlic, spring onions and leeks and cook, stirring, for 4 minutes or until leeks are soft.

2 Add red capsicum and spinach and cook, stirring, for 3 minutes or until spinach wilts. Drain off liquid.

3 Transfer vegetable mixture to a large bowl, add ricotta cheese, sweetcorn and paprika and mix well to combine.

4 Spoon filling into cannelloni tubes and place tubes side-by-side in a greased large ovenproof dish. Set aside.

5 To make sauce, heat oil in a saucepan over a medium heat. Add onion and cook, stirring, for 3 minutes or until onion is soft. Stir in tomato puree and wine, bring to simmering and simmer for 4 minutes. Pour sauce over cannelloni tubes, sprinkle with mozzarella cheese and bake for 40 minutes or until pasta is tender and cheese is golden.

Serves 4

12 instant (no precooking required) cannelloni tubes

250g mozzarella cheese, grated

Leek and spinach filling

2 teaspoons olive oil

1 clove garlic, crushed

2 spring onions, finely chopped

2 leeks, thinly sliced

1 red capsicum, sliced

1 bunch English spinach, chopped

200g ricotta cheese, drained

315g canned creamed sweetcorn

2 teaspoons ground paprika

Tomato sauce

1 teaspoon olive oil

1 onion, chopped

440g canned tomato puree

2 tablespoons dry white wine

Bean sprout omelette

Filling

30g butter

2 tablespoons grated fresh ginger

4 tablespoons bean sprouts

4 chives, finely chopped

Omelette

1 teaspoon butter

2 eggs

2 teaspoons water

freshly ground black pepper

Serves 1

1 To make filling, melt butter in a small frying pan. Add ginger, bean sprouts and chives and cook for 1 minute. Remove from pan and keep warm.

2 To make omelette, melt butter in a small frying pan. Lightly whisk together eggs and water and season with pepper. Pour into pan and cook over medium heat. Continually draw the edge of the omelette in with a fork during cooking until no liquid remains and the omelette is lightly set.

3 Sprinkle the bean sprout mixture over the omelette and fold in half. Slip onto a plate and serve immediately.

Spicy buckwheat noodles

500g buckwheat noodles

1 tablespoon olive oil

3 cloves garlic, crushed

2 fresh red chillies, seeded and chopped

200g rocket leaves, stems removed and leaves shredded

2 tomatoes, chopped

Serves 4

1 Cook noodles in boiling water in a large saucepan following packet directions. Drain, set aside and keep warm.

2 Heat oil in a frying pan. Add garlic and cook over a medium heat, stirring, for 1 minute. Add chillies, rocket and tomatoes and cook for 2 minutes longer or until rocket wilts. Toss vegetable mixture with noodles and serve immediately.

Note: If rocket is unavailable you can use watercress instead. For a complete meal, accompany with a tossed green salad and wholemeal bread rolls.

Chickpea and pasta patties

- *75g tiny pasta shapes*
- *440g canned chickpeas, drained and rinsed*
- *½ cup flour*
- *1 onion, chopped*
- *6 tablespoons chopped fresh parsley*
- *1 clove garlic, crushed*
- *1 teaspoon ground cumin*
- *¼ teaspoon dried chilli flakes*
- *2 tablespoons lemon juice*
- *1 egg, lightly beaten*
- *seasoned flour*
- *vegetable oil for shallow frying*

Makes 14 patties

1 Cook pasta in boiling water in a large saucepan following packet directions. Drain, rinse under cold water and drain again.

2 Place chickpeas in a bowl and mash. Add pasta, flour, onion, parsley, garlic, cumin, chilli flakes, lemon juice and egg and mix to combine. Cover and refrigerate for 1 hour.

3 Divide mixture into 14 portions and shape each into a patty. Roll each patty in seasoned flour to coat.

4 Heat 1cm oil in a frying pan over a medium heat and cook patties, in batches, for 3 minutes each side or until golden and heated through. Drain on absorbent kitchen paper.

Fettuccine with corn sauce

1 Cook pasta in boiling water in a large saucepan following packet directions. Drain, set aside and keep warm.

2 To make sauce, heat oil in a saucepan over a medium heat, add red capsicum and cook, stirring, for 2 minutes or until pepper is soft. Stir in sweet corn, water, chilli sauce, coriander and black pepper to taste and cook for 2 minutes longer or until sauce is hot. Spoon sauce over pasta and toss to combine.

500 g fresh fettuccine

Corn and coriander sauce

1 tablespoon olive oil

1 red capsicum, chopped

440g canned creamed sweet corn

1/4 cup water

2 teaspoons hot chilli sauce

2 tablespoons chopped fresh coriander

freshly ground black pepper

Serves 4

Forest mushroom pasta

375g pasta of your choice

2 teaspoons vegetable oil

1 clove garlic, crushed

750g mixed mushrooms

White sauce

30g butter

2 tablespoons flour

2 cups milk

1/2 teaspoon ground nutmeg

freshly ground black pepper

Serves 4

1 Cook pasta in boiling water in a large saucepan following packet directions. Drain, set aside and keep warm.

2 To make sauce, melt butter in a saucepan over a medium heat. Stir in flour and cook, stirring, for 1 minute. Remove pan from heat and whisk in milk. Return pan to heat and cook, stirring, until sauce boils and thickens. Stir in nutmeg and season to taste with black pepper. Add sauce to pasta and mix to combine. Set aside and keep warm.

3 Heat oil in a frying pan over a medium heat. Add garlic and mushrooms and cook, stirring, for 4 minutes or until mushrooms are soft. To serve, top pasta with mushroom mixture.

Ravioli with walnut sauce

750g cheese and spinach ravioli

Walnut sauce

200g walnuts

½ bunch fresh basil, leaves removed and stems discarded

45g butter, softened

45g grated Parmesan cheese

freshly ground black pepper

100mL olive oil

155mL cream (double)

Serves 4

1 Cook ravioli in boiling water in a large saucepan following packet directions. Drain, set aside and keep warm.

2 To make sauce, place walnuts and basil in a food processor or blender and process until finely chopped. Add butter, Parmesan cheese and black pepper to taste. With machine running, slowly add oil and cream and process until it is just combined. To serve, spoon sauce over pasta and toss.

Chilli bean rolls

315g prepared puff pastry

1 egg, lightly beaten

Chilli bean filling

440g canned red kidney beans, rinsed and drained

4 tablespoons tomato paste

2 tablespoons mild chilli sauce

60g grated tasty cheese (mature Cheddar)

1 teaspoon ground cumin

1 teaspoon ground coriander

Makes 8

1 Roll out pastry to 3mm thick and cut into eight 10 x 15cm rectangles. Set aside.

2 To make filling, place red kidney beans, tomato paste, chilli sauce, cheese, cumin and coriander in a bowl. Mash lightly to combine.

3 Place a spoonful of filling lengthwise down the centre of each pastry rectangle. Fold edges over and roll to encase filling.

4 Place rolls on greased baking trays, brush with egg and bake for 20 minutes or until pastry is puffed and golden.

Lentil and cheese loaf

1 Bring a large saucepan of water to the boil. Add lentils, reduce heat and simmer for 20 minutes or until tender. Drain.

2 Place lentils, cheese, salmon (if using), spring onions, parsley, lemon juice, paprika, egg and cream in a bowl and mix well to combine. Spoon mixture into a greased 11 x 21cm loaf tin and bake for 40 minutes or until firm.

3 To make dressing, place mayonnaise, sun-dried tomatoes, basil and black pepper to taste in a food processor or blender and process until well combined. Serve with loaf.

155g red lentils

125g grated tasty cheese (mature Cheddar)

220g canned salmon, drained and flaked (optional)

4 spring onions, sliced

3 tablespoons chopped fresh parsley

1 tablespoon lemon juice

1 teaspoon paprika

1 egg, lightly beaten

1/4 cup cream (double)

Sun-dried tomato dressing

1/2 cup mayonnaise

6 sun-dried tomatoes, chopped

1 tablespoon chopped fresh basil

freshly ground black pepper

Serves 4

Potato and pumpkin tagine

500g peeled and deseeded pumpkin

4 medium potatoes

400g canned tomatoes in juice

1 cup vegetable stock

6 dried apricots

1/4 teaspoon ground cinnamon

1/4 teaspoon ground ginger

1/4 teaspoon cayenne pepper

1/4 cup lemon juice

1 tablespoon honey

Serves 6–8

1 Cut pumpkin into 4cm chunks. Peel potatoes and cut into eight large even-sized pieces. Cook pumpkin and potatoes in stock and tomatoes in their juice.

2 Chop apricots. Add cinnamon, ginger, cayenne pepper, lemon juice, honey and apricots. Cover and simmer for 25 to 30 minutes. Serve with rice or couscous.

Vegetable frittata

500g fresh vegetables of your choice

2 tablespoons light olive oil

4 eggs

salt

freshly ground black pepper

Serves 4

1 Trim vegetables and cut into pieces. Heat oil in a large frying pan. Add vegetables and cook over a low heat until vegetables begin to wilt.

2 Beat eggs in a bowl and add salt and pepper. Pour eggs into pan. Cook frittata until lightly browned on one side, then carefully turn and cook second side. Serve cut into wedges.

Lentil frittata

155g red lentils

2 teaspoons vegetable oil

2 leeks, chopped

20 English spinach leaves, shredded

6 zucchini, sliced

250g smoked cod or haddock, cooked and flesh flaked (optional)

6 eggs, lightly beaten

$^3/_4$ cup natural yoghurt

2 tablespoons chopped fresh chervil or parsley

freshly ground black pepper

Serves 4

1 Bring a large saucepan of water to the boil. Add lentils, reduce heat and simmer for 20 minutes or until tender. Drain and set aside.

2 Heat oil in a frying pan over a medium heat, add leeks and cook, stirring, for 4 minutes or until soft and golden. Add spinach, zucchini and smoked fish (if using) and cook for 3 minutes longer. Stir in lentils and mix to combine.

3 Place eggs, yoghurt, chervil or parsley and black pepper to taste in a bowl and whisk to combine. Pour egg mixture over vegetables in pan and cook over a low heat for 6 minutes or until frittata is almost set. Place pan under a preheated hot grill and cook for 2 minutes or until top is golden.

Rice and apricot pilaf

3 tablespoons oil or butter

1 large onion, finely chopped

1½ cups rice

4 cups hot water

salt and freshly ground pepper

2 tablespoons lemon juice

2 tablespoons parsley, finely chopped

210g dried apricots

2 tablespoons raisins

60g almonds, blanched and toasted

Serves 4

1 Heat oil or butter in a large saucepan and fry the onion until pale golden in colour. Add rice, stir for 30 seconds to coat with oil.

2 Add hot water, salt, pepper, lemon juice and parsley. Cover and simmer for 10 minutes.

3 Stir in apricots, raisins and almonds and simmer for 5 minutes more. Remove from heat and allow to stand, covered, for 5 minutes before serving to plump the rice.

Vegetable curry with chutney

Rhubarb chutney

500g rhubarb, chopped
1 tablespoon grated fresh ginger
1 fresh green chilli, chopped
1 tablespoon black mustard seeds
125g brown sugar
1 cup white vinegar
60g currants

Curry

2 teaspoons vegetable oil
1 teaspoon ground cumin
1 tablespoon curry paste
2 onions, chopped
2 potatoes, finely chopped
200g cauliflower, cut into florets
200g broccoli, cut into florets
150g green beans, halved
1 red capsicum, chopped
2 zucchini, chopped
200mL coconut milk
200mL vegetable stock

1 To make chutney, place rhubarb, ginger, chilli, mustard seeds, sugar, vinegar and currants in a saucepan and cook over a medium heat, stirring occasionally, for 30 minutes or until mixture is soft and pulpy.

2 To make curry, heat oil in a large saucepan, add cumin, curry paste and onions and cook, stirring, for 3 minutes or until onions are soft. Add potatoes, cauliflower, broccoli, beans, red capsicum, zucchini, coconut milk and stock and bring to the boil. Reduce heat and simmer, stirring occasionally, for 25 to 35 minutes or until vegetables are tender. Serve curry with rhubarb chutney.

Note: Serve this curry with jasmine or basmati rice. Rhubarb chutney can be stored in sterilised airtight jars for several months.

Serves 4

Sweet potato and tofu curry

1 tablespoon peanut oil

1 teaspoon chilli oil (optional)

315g firm tofu, cut into 1 cm thick slices

1 1/2 cups coconut cream

1 cup vegetable stock

2 teaspoons Thai red curry paste

375g sweet potato, cut into 2 cm cubes

2 teaspoons palm or brown sugar

1 tablespoon Thai fish sauce (nam pla)

2 teaspoons lime juice

60g fresh basil leaves

Serves 4

1 Heat peanut oil and chilli oil (if using) in a wok or large saucepan over a medium heat. Add tofu and stir-fry until brown on all sides. Remove, drain on absorbent kitchen paper and set aside.

2 Using absorbent kitchen paper, wipe wok or saucepan clean, then add coconut cream and stock and bring to the boil. Stir in curry paste and cook for 3 to 4 minutes or until fragrant.

3 Add sweet potato, cover and cook over a medium heat for 8 to 10 minutes or until sweet potato is almost cooked.

4 Stir in sugar, fish sauce and lime juice and cook for 4 to 5 minutes longer or until sweet potato is tender. Stir in basil.

Curried vegetables

- *500g small chat potatoes, cut in half*
- *4 tablespoons oil*
- *400g onions, peeled and thinly sliced*
- *250g green zucchini*
- *250g yellow squash, cut in half*
- *250g stringless beans, topped, tailed and cut in half*
- *3 tablespoons butter or ghee*
- *2 tablespoons curry paste*
- *¾ cup raisins, soaked for 10 minutes*
- *1 red capsicum, cut into 2½cm squares*
- *60g pistachio nuts*
- *1 tablespoon sunflower seeds*

Serves 4–5

1 Boil potatoes in boiling, salted water until just tender. Drain and set aside. Heat oil in a frying pan, add onions and toss to coat with oil. Reduce heat, cover and allow to cook on low heat until onions become soft. Remove lid, increase heat and fry, stirring frequently until the onions are well browned.

2 Parboil the zucchini, squash and beans in boiling, salted water for 2 minutes. Drain and immediately cover with cold water. Leave 30 seconds, then drain well.

3 Heat butter or ghee in a large frying pan, add curry paste and cook, stirring, until fragrant. Add potatoes, cook, tossing around the pan until brown and crisp. Add parboiled vegetables, raisins and capsicum. Stir-fry well to heat through and coat with curry paste.

4 Toss through pistachio nuts and sunflower seeds. Remove to a serving platter and top with fried onions.

Coconut vegetable curry

1 Heat oil in a large saucepan over a medium heat. Add onion and garlic and cook, stirring, for 5 minutes or until onion softens slightly. Add curry and chilli powders and cook, stirring, for 1 minute longer.

2 Stir in coconut cream, water, potatoes, sweet potato, peas, pasta and lemon juice and bring to the boil. Reduce heat and simmer, stirring occasionally, for 20 minutes or until vegetables and pasta are cooked. Stir in coriander and serve.

1 tablespoon vegetable oil

1 onion, sliced

1 clove garlic, crushed

1 tablespoon hot curry powder

1/4 teaspoon chilli powder

1 1/2 cups coconut cream

3 cups water

2 potatoes, cubed

250g sweet potato, cubed

125g shelled fresh or frozen peas

125g risoni or orzo pasta (small rice shapes)

2 teaspoons lemon juice

1 tablespoon chopped fresh coriander

Serves 4

Vegetable and apple curry

3 eggplants, cut into 1 cm slices

salt

1/3 cup vegetable oil

3 apples, peeled and cored, cut into thick slices

2 tablespoons curry paste

1 teaspoon ground cinnamon

2 whole cloves

1 1/2 cups coconut milk

1 tablespoon lemon juice

45g sultanas

1 tablespoon chopped fresh mint

1 tablespoon chopped fresh coriander

Serves 4

1 Place eggplant slices in a colander set over a bowl, sprinkle with salt and stand for 20 minutes. Rinse under cold water and pat dry with absorbent kitchen paper.

2 Heat 2 tablespoons oil in a frying pan over a medium heat and cook eggplant and apples in batches for 5 minutes or until brown. Remove and drain on absorbent kitchen paper.

3 Heat remaining oil in pan over a medium heat, add curry paste, cinnamon and cloves and cook for 2 minutes or until fragrant. Stir in coconut milk, lemon juice, sultanas, mint and coriander, bring to simmering and simmer, stirring occasionally, for 15 minutes.

4 Return eggplant and apples to pan and simmer for 15 minutes longer or until tender.

Eggplant and basil stir-fry

3 eggplants, halved lengthways and cut into 1cm thick slices

salt

1 tablespoon vegetable oil

2 onions, cut into thin wedges, layers separated

3 fresh red chillies, chopped

2 cloves garlic, sliced

1 stalk fresh lemongrass, chopped, or 1/2 teaspoon dried lemongrass, soaked in hot water until soft

250g green beans, trimmed

1 cup coconut cream

45g basil leaves

Serves 6

1 Place eggplant in a colander, sprinkle with salt and set aside for 20 minutes. Rinse under cold water and pat dry with absorbent kitchen paper.

2 Heat oil in a wok or frying pan over a high heat, add onions, chillies, garlic and lemongrass and stir-fry for 3 minutes. Add eggplant, beans and coconut cream and stir-fry for 5 minutes or until eggplant are tender. Stir in basil just before serving.

Tofu with peaches and snow peas

375g tub of tofu

½ cup flour, seasoned

3 tablespoons oil

1 large onion, cut into rings

1 cm piece fresh ginger root, peeled

1 clove garlic, peeled

300g snow peas, topped and tailed

⅓ cup dry white wine

200g packet dried peaches

3 teaspoons soy sauce

2 teaspoons sugar

Serves 2–3

1 Cut tofu into six cubes and toss with seasoned flour.

2 Heat oil in a large frying pan and fry onion rings until golden. Remove onion rings.

3 Add ginger and garlic, fry for 30 seconds to flavour the oil then remove. Add tofu cubes and fry until golden on all sides, turning with tongs. Remove and drain on kitchen paper.

4 Fry snow peas for about 1 minute or to desired crispness. Remove.

5 Pour wine into pan and place in the peaches. Simmer 1 minute, turn peaches. Add soy and sugar. Swirl pan to mix.

6 Pile tofu, snow peas and peaches onto plates. Pour over the sauce and top with onion rings

Crispy noodles with vegetables

1 Heat oil in a wok until a cube of bread dropped in browns in 50 seconds, then deep-fry noodles in batches until puffed and crisp. Drain noodles on absorbent kitchen paper.

2 Drain all but 2 tablespoons of oil from wok, then add spring onions, ginger and garlic and stir-fry for 2 minutes.

3 Add snow peas, carrots, tofu and red capsicum and stir-fry for 3 minutes. Add mushrooms and stir-fry for 1 minute.

4 Stir in chilli, sugar, chilli sauce and lemon juice and bring to the boil. Remove wok from heat, add fried noodles and coriander leaves and toss to combine. Serve immediately.

Note: Deep-fried tofu can be found in the refrigerator section of Asian food stores. Purchased deep-fried tofu should be simmered in boiling water before using, as this removes the excess oil. You can make your own deep-fried tofu by cutting pressed (firm) tofu into squares then deep-frying it.

Serves 4

vegetable oil for deep-frying

125g dried rice vermicelli noodles, broken into small pieces

3 spring onions, sliced

2 tablespoon finely grated fresh ginger

2 cloves garlic, crushed

150g snow peas

2 carrots, sliced

125g deep-fried tofu, cut into strips

1 red capsicum, sliced

125g oyster mushrooms

1 teaspoon chopped fresh red chilli

1 tablespoon brown sugar

2 tablespoons chilli sauce

1 tablespoon lemon juice

1 large bunch fresh coriander

Chinese vegetable medley

- 1 medium Chinese turnip
- 1 carrot
- 2 onions
- 2 sticks celery
- ½ Chinese cabbage
- ½ cup water
- 2 tablespoons soy sauce
- 1 tablespoon sesame oil
- ½ teaspoon sugar
- ¼ cup roasted cashew nuts

Serves 4

1 Peel turnip, carrot and onions. Cut turnip and carrot into thin matchstick-sized pieces. Slice onions thinly. Trim celery and slice. Wash cabbage and slice thinly.

2 Bring water to the boil in a wok or frying pan. Toss turnip, carrot, onion and celery in boiling water for 2 minutes. Add cabbage and cook for 1 minute. Drain vegetables well, then return to wok.

3 Add soy sauce, sesame oil, sugar and cashew nuts to wok and toss through. Serve immediately.

Pumpkin with chilli and lime

500g peeled and deseeded pumpkin

50g butter

1 teaspoon prepared minced chilli

½ teaspoon grated lime rind

2 tablespoons lime juice

1 tablespoon chopped parsley

Serves 4

1 Cut pumpkin into 1cm wide lengths like French fries. Cook in boiling salted water for 3 to 5 minutes or until just soft. Drain.

2 Melt butter in a saucepan. Add chilli, lime rind and juice to pan. Pour over pumpkin. Serve sprinkled with parsley.

Ratatouille

- 1 eggplant
- salt
- 1 onion
- 3 cloves garlic
- 1 tablespoon oil
- 1 tablespoon tomato paste
- 4 tomatoes
- 1 red capsicums
- 1 green capsicums
- 4 zucchini
- 1 teaspoon dried rosemary
- 1/2 teaspoon thyme
- 1 bay leaf
- 1 tablespoon chopped parsley

Serves 4–6

1 Trim ends from eggplant. Cut into slices and sprinkle with salt. Set aside while preparing remaining ingredients. Peel onion and chop finely. Crush, peel and chop garlic.

2 Heat oil in a frying pan or flameproof casserole dish. Sauté onion and garlic for 3 to 5 minutes, or until onion is clear. Mix onion, garlic and tomato paste together in casserole dish. Dice tomatoes. Deseed and slice red and green capsicums. Trim zucchini and cut into 1cm slices.

3 Add tomatoes, capsicums, zucchini, rosemary, thyme and bay leaf to casserole dish. Wash salt from eggplant and cut each slice into quarters. Add to casserole dish. Mix gently. Cover and cook at 180°C for 1 to 1 1/4 hours. Serve sprinkled with chopped parsley.

French beans with tomato and garlic sauce

400g canned tomatoes in juice

500g fresh or frozen French beans

2 cloves garlic

2 tablespoons light olive oil

1 teaspoon dried basil

salt

freshly ground black pepper

Serves 4

1 Cut tomatoes into large pieces. If using fresh beans, wash them and snap off ends. Crush, peel and chop garlic.

2 Heat olive oil in a large frying pan. Add garlic and cook until golden. Add tomatoes and beans and cook for 10 minutes or until beans are tender but firm. Remove beans with a slotted spoon and place on a dish.

3 Bring tomato mixture to the boil and cook until sauce thickens. Stir in basil. Return beans to pan and serve. Season with salt and freshly ground black pepper.

Bok choy with oyster sauce

600g bok choy or bar choy

1 clove garlic

1 tablespoon toasted sesame seeds

2 tablespoons oyster sauce

snow pea sprouts

Serves 2

1 Wash bok choy and separate leaves. Crush, peel and chop garlic. Sprinkle garlic over base of a bamboo or metal steamer. Place bok choy on top.

2 Cover and place in a wok or frying pan or, if using a European-style steamer, over a saucepan of water. Pour enough water into the frying pan to come quarter of the way up the side of the bamboo steamer. Steam for about 5 minutes or until bok choy looks wilted.

3 Place on a serving platter. Sprinkle over sesame seeds, pour over oyster sauce and garnish with snow pea sprouts.

Note: If you would prefer a different flavour for this dish, try an Asian sauce like hoisin or any of the huge variety of Asian sauces that take your fancy.

Coconut cauli

- *1 small cauliflower*
- *400mL canned coconut cream*
- *½ teaspoon ground chilli*
- *1 teaspoon turmeric*
- *1 teaspoon ground coriander*
- *1 teaspoon ground ginger*
- *½ teaspoon sugar*
- *1 teaspoon salt*
- *1 teaspoon grated lime rind*
- *2 tablespoons lime juice*
- *lime slices*

Serves 4–6

1 Wash and trim cauliflower. Leave whole. Place coconut cream, chilli, turmeric, coriander, ginger, sugar and salt in a saucepan large enough to hold the cauliflower. Bring to the boil. Place cauliflower in the liquid.

2 Cover and cook for 15 minutes or until cauliflower is just cooked. Mix in lime rind and juice. Serve with coconut mixture poured over cauliflower. Garnish with lime slices.

Stir-fry cabbage with peanuts

2 cloves garlic

½ large cabbage

1 onion

1 tablespoon peanut oil

pinch ground chilli

1 teaspoon yellow mustard seeds

¼ cup roasted peanuts

2 tablespoons sherry

1 tablespoon soy sauce

Serves 4–6

1 Crush, peel and chop garlic. Wash cabbage, remove core and shred cabbage coarsely. Peel onion and cut into rings.

2 Heat oil in a wok or frying pan. Stir-fry garlic and onion for 2 to 3 minutes. Add chilli and mustard seeds and stir-fry until mustard seeds begin to pop.

3 Add cabbage and peanuts and stir-fry over a high heat for 2 to 3 minutes until cabbage wilts but is still bright green. Add sherry and soy sauce. Cook for a further minute. Serve immediately.

Carrots with vinegar and oregano

4 medium carrots

3 cloves garlic

2 tablespoons light olive oil

½ cup wine vinegar

1 teaspoon dried oregano

½ teaspoon prepared minced chilli

½ teaspoon sugar

salt

freshly ground black pepper

Serves 4

1 Peel carrots and cut into 5mm rounds. Cook carrots in boiling salted water for 5 minutes. Drain well. Crush, peel and sliver garlic.

2 Heat oil in a large frying pan. Sauté garlic and carrots for 2 minutes, stirring frequently. Add vinegar, oregano, chilli, sugar, salt and pepper and cook for about 10 minutes or until all liquid has evaporated. Serve warm or at room temperature.

Stir-fried broccoli with orange and ginger

500g broccoli

1 tablespoon peanut oil

2 tablespoons finely chopped root ginger

1 teaspoon grated orange rind

1/4 cup orange juice

1 teaspoon stir-fry seasoning

1/2 teaspoon Tabasco sauce

2 tablespoons chopped chives

Serves 4

1 Trim broccoli and cut into florets. Heat oil in a wok or frying pan. Stir-fry broccoli and ginger for 2 to 3 minutes. Add orange rind, juice, stir-fry seasoning and Tabasco sauce.

2 Bring to the boil, cover and simmer for 5 minutes or until broccoli is just tender and liquid has evaporated. Toss chives through and serve immediately.

Note: Substitute any other green vegetable for broccoli if you prefer.

Asparagus and red capsicum stir-fry

500g fresh asparagus
1 small onion
2 cloves garlic
2 red capsicums
2 tablespoons peanut oil
½ cup water
1 tablespoon sugar
1 teaspoon Szechuan seasoning

Serves 4

1 Wash asparagus and snap off tough ends. Cut spears into 3cm lengths. Peel onion and chop finely. Crush, peel and finely chop garlic. Deseed capsicums and cut into thin strips.

2 Heat oil in a wok or frying pan and stir-fry onion and garlic for 3 to 5 minutes or until clear but not coloured. Add water, then asparagus and capsicums. Add sugar and bring to the boil.

3 Cook for about 3 minutes or until asparagus is tender. Drain. Toss Szechuan seasoning through. Serve immediately.

Spicy *eggplant* and potatoes

1 medium eggplant

2 large potatoes

2 onions

1 clove garlic

¼ cup peanut oil

1 tablespoon finely chopped root ginger

360g jar Massaman curry sauce

1 tablespoon chopped fresh coriander

Serves 4

1 Wash eggplant and cut into 2cm cubes. Peel potatoes and cut into 2cm cubes. Peel onions and cut into eighths. Crush, peel and chop garlic.

2 Heat oil in a wok or frying pan and stir-fry potatoes, onion, garlic and ginger for 5 minutes. Add eggplant and stir-fry for another 5 minutes. Add curry sauce and mix.

3 Bring to the boil and cook for 15 minutes or until potatoes are tender. Serve garnished with coriander.

Garlic and rosemary potatoes

6 medium potatoes

4 cloves garlic

¼ cup light olive oil

1½ teaspoons dried rosemary

freshly ground black pepper

Serves 4

1 Peel potatoes and cut into 2cm cubes. Crush, peel and finely chop garlic. Heat oil in a roasting pan. Add potatoes, garlic and rosemary.

2 Bake at 190°C for about 30 minutes or until potatoes are cooked, turning potatoes frequently during cooking. Arrange on a serving plate and grind black pepper over.

Baked potato croquettes

4 medium potatoes

2 eggs

2 tablespoons sour cream

1 tablespoon chopped parsley

½ teaspoon salt

1 tablespoon water

1 tablespoon cornflour

about 2 cups dried breadcrumbs

Serves 6

1 Peel potatoes and cut into even-sized pieces. Cook in boiling, salted water for 15 to 20 minutes or until soft. Drain and mash. Beat one egg and sour cream into mashed potato. Mix in parsley and salt. Refrigerate for 30 minutes.

2 Lightly beat second egg with water and cornflour. Work the potato mixture into quarter-cup-sized oval croquette shapes. Dip in egg, then breadcrumbs to coat.

3 Place croquettes in a greased roasting dish and bake at 180°C for 20 to 30 minutes, turning halfway through cooking. Serve with a fresh tomato salsa or as a meal accompaniment.